life and how to do it

Tara Leaver

with gratitude
to Pauline Leger,
for her design skills and endless patience

ISBN-13: 978-1547295043
ISBN-10: 154729504X

Contents

Introduction

Like many creative endeavours, these poems took both several years and a series of brief moments to come into being. Mostly the poems write themselves. Sometimes I begin with a kernel of an idea and see what happens when I let it unfold on the paper. Sometimes I am so full of something it overflows into words that do their best to describe the experience, often inadequately. Words can only take us so far. My hope is that you will not read these particular words as mine, but as ours, or simply as words that carry a message for you.

I don't consider myself a poet in any kind of official capacity, but I am a lover of words. I like to roll words and phrases around in my mouth, mind and heart. Words are a way to play in the world, a way to translate celebration, despair, and everything in between into something shareable, through which we can connect.

These poems are about the human experience and its paradoxes; knowing that you know and feeling like you don't, heartbreak, mending, moments of clarity, noticing things and trying to make sense of them, love, dreams, growing pains, the seductive pull of the dark. I have learned that my most intensely personal experiences are not personal at all, but universal; in expressing them I acknowledge what being human can feel like, and the experiences that come with this gig. More significantly, the words act as a permission giver or 'reminder-er' of how we can remember something beyond our perceived limitations and 'come home'. I've noticed that the relief in expressing all this is always matched by the relief in reading it and the feeling engendered of yes, me too. *Listen*, the poems say, *we are alone, yes, but we are also not alone.*

I had one of those Divine moments of crystal clarity the other day, one that lasted just a few seconds but felt like an opening into Truth. It came in the form of a deeply felt experience, in my body and heart and mind, of how we all, every last one of us, just want to be seen, which is to say we just want to be loved, exactly as we are. And that it makes no sense to me to be here and not at least attempt to offer that to my fellow humans-who-are-me in whatever way I can. These poems are one way for me to do that; to say *yes, I know what it's like to be human and see? We are the same, deep down where it matters.*

My wish for you is that somewhere in these pages you feel that moment of recognition and the relief or expansive joy that comes with it, even just for a moment. I've included some of my sea photographs, to act as pauses in which to soak up the words and whatever meaning or healing they have for you. The sea is my home, {I was almost certainly a mermaid in a previous life,} my reminder of where I really live, beyond the perceived limits of my body and what the Tao Te Ching calls the ten thousand things. My hope is that in these pages you will find glimpses of that too. When we learn to string them together we find we are home all the time.

I'm still learning, of course; this is not a book of answers {the title is one of my secret jokes:)}, and I'm pretty sure I'm not enlightened yet. :) If anything it will probably beget more questions, and I think that's a good thing. We must keep asking questions until the necessity for them no longer exists, by which I mean that we go beyond both questions and answers to the place of which I've had glimpses, of home. If you enjoy the book, please share it. As Ram Dass so beautifully put it, 'we are all just walking each other home', so let's use whatever means available.

With love
Tara
England, June 2017

You Are a Blessing

Like light that sparkles the water
like warm sweet sips on an arctic day
like pink blooms dancing
or a breeze brushing skin

You are a blessing.
Do you know what that means?
Not that you are something
you fear you can't live up to
that feels like a weight
or something that doesn't belong to you.

It means your simple existence
is sparkles on water to the light starved
warmth spreading inside after the stinging cold
colour in someone's leaden day
or a promise of pleasure whispered over bare shoulders.

You are a blessing.
It doesn't matter how
or whether {yes}
or when {always}
What matters is
that you know it
so that you will always be you
releasing your gifts
like seeds on the wind.

The Gathering

They're going to tell you
That what you need is this:

Stuff that looks like something
Car shaped
House shaped
Career shaped
And love:
Love will look like this
It will fit in a box
That looks like everyone else's
And if it doesn't
You will be judged.
Silently, if you're lucky.

You must gather.
Call these things to you
Stack them up around you
And eventually you will have
Enough things that
In their proximity to you
Will give you a shape
Will show the world who you are
And {they don't tell you this}
Then you will know who you are, too.

So you dutifully gathered.
You stacked and built and made.
You created a shape.
It looked like you.
It talked like you.
It did the kind of things you might do. But secretly in the dark
It didn't FEEL like you.

May I make a suggestion.

If the shape that is you
Is uncomfortable
{and most likely it feels too small}
Then consider
That you just misunderstood
The gathering.

Try this on for size.
Drop all the things.
I don't mean run away
Or abandon your loved ones
Or give it all up and live in a cave. Necessarily.
Being willing to let go
Doesn't mean you will have to.

So drop all the things
That are not you
And turn the other way.
The act of releasing
Is itself a turning in.
At first you may see nothing
{your fear of this was why you stacked the things}
Be patient.
Begin to gather
The pieces of your real self
You've scattered far and wide.
Call them home.

Rinse and repeat.
Gather, release.
Call in, let go.
Over and over.
Daily. Hourly. When you remember.

And look!
See who is emerging
From the rubble of the things
That were not you,
That you were not.

It looks like you
Sounds like you
But the most important part
It FEELS like you.
And you glow
And people notice but can't quite….
And everything looks the same, and different.
And you step out of the wreckage
Ungathered.
Renewed.
Free.

God's Casino

When you ask for something
God says
I'll see your desire
And I'll raise it
A thousandfold.

You are so busy
Trying to get what you want
That you forget
it might already have arrived
in unexpected packaging.

When the desire is there but everything else is louder

When you feel the pull
that tug inside
that has no words
but insists
like a mute but stubborn child,
I want this.
I want it.
Want it.

The only way

The ONLY way
to silence it
to feel the peace
that comes with
a sudden stopping
is to listen
and respond.

That mute caller
you're ignoring
sidelining
not now-ing
latering
squashing

is you.

How long can you
ignore yourself?

Sure, a lifetime
but how tired you will be
at the end

from all that
unanswered wanting
how hollow
how unfulfilled.

Better to be filled
with things tried
with experiments that
didn't work
with colour
and texture
and the song of joy
your body sings
when you
answer the call

than to be filled
with regret
that you never listened
because the later
that never comes
always seemed
like a better time.

Icebergs

We are icebergs.

So little seen
Vast and majestic beneath the surface.

We bump and collide
Surprised by the invisible bulk
Of secret selves
Revealed.

I take comfort
In my eyes' deception.
There is more to you
And that is the adventure.

Misinterpretations end
Beneath the skin.

We are all the same
In the dark.

Love Poem

You use
your words
to seduce
when beneath
there is nothing
that could
be construed
as the truth.

I was moved.
I let go
and that proved
just a slow
and uneven
descent
we were
evidently
not meant
to last
or to grow.

The bond
that we tied
partly real
edged with lies
or half truths
was too weak
in the end
to survive.
It took me
so long
to see
and to feel
what was
actually real:

that you leaned
and I reeled
and keeled
over.

I chose
the bright side
and denied
the misgivings
that prodded
inside.
I lied –
to myself.
Not to you.
It was true,
all the love
that I carried
for you.
For two.
And you knew.

We both
had a dream
and it seemed
to be shared.
I know
we both cared.
But the friendship
began
to snag
at the seams
when I learned
that your words
do not show
what you mean.

And that I
not prepared
to declare
what was true
did not dare
to admit
it was through.

And though
I fell far
and the scars
from the shards
still remain
in my brain
and my heart,
I know now
that the love
that I gave
was all mine
wasn't lost
or declined
it was just
misaligned.
It still shines
from inside.
I can find it
most days
if I try.

Shouting in the Library

It seems to me
That everyone's always talking about
Speaking Your Truth

And how important it is
if you want
to be happy

And it's not that I don't agree
but when I do it
or think about doing it
sometimes
it feels like

shouting in the library

You Don't Have To

you don't have to be 'fixed' in a certain amount of time
{you are not broken, anyway}
it's a process, and tomorrow is ok
so is next year

you don't have to be cheerful and grateful all day long
{but you can be thankful for that, if you like}

you can lie on the kitchen floor,
wracked with sobs and that big hole in your chest gaping,
all morning long;
and go out for tea with a friend and laugh all afternoon.

yes you can change, moment to moment

you don't have to answer "how are you?"
fine or not fine
you don't have to answer that question at all.

you don't have to be afraid -
of the day ahead
of emptiness
of space
or grey skies.
none of these things can hurt you, unless you say they can.

you don't have to prove anything
achieve anything
'do something constructive'

you don't have to always make sense
you don't have to do it because you said you would

there aren't any rules, not really
there isn't a right order to things
No One is waiting to humiliate you when you make a mistake
you can go for a walk after dark
buy only what food you feel like eating
stare into space, indefinitely.
skip breakfast, eat two lunches and have cereal for supper

you don't have to reply straight away
you don't have to make sure everyone's ok
you don't have to do the thing that makes sense
you don't have to wait and see
you don't have to jump straight in.

look at your life. look at your life.
that's right, it's yours! what a gift!
you don't have to listen to what they think it should look like.

that's why you were given a drum
for your own rhythm
a body, for your own dance
and wings
because you can fly,
even if today you don't remember how.

One Day

There's something I'd like to do.
A secret dream (or two),
living in my pocket.
It shines
from all the times
I took it out
to cherish it,
look forward to it,
relish it,
careful not to drop it.

My beautiful dream.
So big and so small.
One day I'll do it, be it, see it.
One day, when…

But wait, she said.
When is one day?
That fictional, distant, horizon-shaped day
when the stars will align
in just the right way?

That day never comes
my darling. Don't wait.
'One day' is always one step away,
it's just a delay.

One day
is
today.

Remember This

When you feel small, pinched, boxed in
by thoughts that seem to choose themselves

Remember this:
You are not this body.
The body could never contain you.
You are bigger than anything you can
imagine.

You can choose.
You *can* choose.
You can *choose*.

When the woo woo isn't working
When the word 'meditation' makes you want
to scream
When going within feels like certain death

Remember this:
Everything is very simple
Breathe
Big, slow, inhale, exhale
Imagine flow
Flow of love, if you like
Through you.

Remember this:
You are a part of everything
It's all you.
Of course your mind doesn't get it.
That's ok,
this one's for your heart.

The Whole Big Beautiful Thing

You can dip your toe in
Make ripples in the water's skin
You can circle the outskirts
Peer over the rim
You can waver on the cusp
Swap love for lust
But you will never know
How your heart can sing
If you hold yourself in
And don't give to yourself
The Whole Big Beautiful Thing

Love scenes with God

When God asks you
to get naked
you can say no
of course
but consider
that this is
the ultimate seduction
and the price you will pay
will be everything
but not in the way
it was with the others
losing yourself
is the goal
not the thing to
fight against
the more you fight
the higher the price
nothing but
total surrender
is enough
to come home.

Woman

I am water
rhythmic
ever changing
and still, the same

Shape shifting goddess
I dissolve and reform
moment to moment

Expectations will not hold

I am river
rushing and violent
smooth and slow
rocks will be caressed
or beaten,
depending

I am ice
hard and cold
best left to melt
in a warm place
quietly
and alone

I am vapour
insubstantial
not really here
trying to grasp me
will prove disappointing

I am rain
unpredictable monsoon torrents
and fleeting soft showers
a million tiny kisses
essence drenched

My oceans teem
with wonders
deadly and beautiful
I sparkle and churn
I will not fit in your tiny cup

I will hold you
while you learn to swim
I will surround you with
unexpected
pockets of warmth
and dazzle you
when I dance in the light

My liquid love
will grow you
maybe drown you
There will be no reining in
or holding back

You must learn to read
the language of water
if you want to know
who I am.

Waking Up

I imagined a moment
so clear, so dazzling
a delicious slap
that would unmask the mystery

and I would be forever changed.

Ha.

The truth of it is
there are glimpses
like the sun
seen from a
speeding train
streaking naked
through the trees
or sparks
that fly from
the teeth of a saw
there and then gone
there and then gone

a fleeting admittance
this tiny idea of a person
erased.

And then always
contraction.
An inbreath
a closing
like a jellyfish
pulsing its way
to the surface
undulating

deceptively effortless
as it pushes upwards

The truth
is everywhere
in the push pull of
the waves
the seasons
the cycles
of the moon
and of women

This is my prayer now
Let me love both
since once does not come
without the other.

Prism

I am a prism
crystal. clear
and then
the light
shines through me
and together
we create rainbows.

Peace Underneath

On the surface of things
Droplets bounce on the water's skin
Rain drums on skylights
The yang drowns out the yin

But deep deep down
Where the soul's hum
Vibrates the cells
And the inky dark
Holds the inner secret light
That's where the treasure lies
In the peace underneath.

Inside is where the jewels are
It's where the dance begins.

Life and how to do it

When they were
giving out the handbooks
about life
and how to do it
I must have been
somewhere else
stargazing probably
or thinking about lunch.

And now I don't know
how anything works
or what to do
when
and how
{and also why}.

But I have a blank notebook
and a sparkly pen
so I think I'll
make my own handbook
and write down for myself
what's good to have for lunch
and what I've learned about stars.

ReCreation

When it broke, it shattered.
Not neatly
With a scar you could touch
A tidy seal to mark the change.

The pieces of me
Crunched underfoot for weeks
The shards reopening the wounds
Over and over.

Now I sometimes find
a tiny glinting fragment
when I'm looking for something else
or sweeping a dark corner
but mostly
all my parts are back where they belong
seamless on the outside
veined within by cracks
each piece glued back together
by hand
one by one.

The Wound

At first you ARE the wound
Bloody and weeping
Raw and ragged at the edges.
You bump against the thoughts that reopen you
That break you apart before the healing can begin
You feel you are dying. You are, partly.
All efforts to comfort
Inside and out
Are plasters.
Achingly inadequate.
The endless strings of words loop and tangle
Oceans pour from you
Until you wonder if somewhere a sea has dried up
Just to keep the world in balance.

Time passes.
You walk forward.
Up and out like a child climbing stairs
One, one, two.
The edges soften.
The wound becomes a bruise
Sometimes you knock it accidentally
And spend some time back in the memory of dying.

Sometimes you poke it
Experimentally, hopefully.
Some days the pain is a shock. Aren't I past this?
Other days it's like touching air

It fades to a soft yellow
Until one day you realise
The pain has evaporated
Leaving a tiny scar
In the shape of a heart.

Requirements

To wait when you don't know
if there's anything to wait for
To trust when you don't know
what you're trusting in or
what will become of
the thing you don't know
and only nebulously sense
To live in the unknowing of
what lies on the other side of
all this

These are the requirements
of a life beyond
the one you thought you'd been given
the one that always seemed somehow
Not Quite Everything
a half measure
a glass half empty
the fullness somewhere just
behind the blind spot
beckoning seduction
invisible finger curved
towards the unseen

Can you afford the toll?
If not turn back now
this gate will lead you places
you're not ready for
But if you hear the calling
from the great beyond
wrapped in mystery
like a gift you must urgently open
then dig deep in your pockets
for patience and trust
and you will find it's
worth the price of admission

What I know about letting go

I always thought
{and let's face it, it's often implied}
that letting go
was something you

do.

And that's why it always felt
like a tease
an invisible carrot
held temptingly out of reach
while I tangled myself
trying
knowing that trying was not the way
and not knowing how else to reach for
that elusive 'just'.

I notice now
that the times of letting go
are not a doing.
There is only opening the door
by having a word
with the Great Benevolence
by handing it up
by admitting I don't know how
to release my anxious grip
on this thing I do not want.

And in collaborating
with the Divine
in the relief of giving it over
to Someone Who Knows What To Do
I just
let
go.

Paradox

How is it possible
to be so filled with light
and still
want the darkness
of the you you used to be
still crave the twisting underside
the worn leather and smoke
the strangely empowering sense
of being misunderstood

How do you reconcile
the elastic stretching
towards the numinous glow
while carrying on a secret love affair
with the dark

What does it mean
to long to be clean
while nursing a drink
in the dark of a bar
and loving the dirt
beneath your fingernails

Why do you want
to crease your brow and dive down
to where the light won't reach
and the seductive velvet
can turn to quicksand
at any moment

Will some part of you be always
Orpheus
turning back, longing
to reach into the place where
the dark alone is all you have
where you find a kind of love
against the odds
a love that always hurts
from endless wanting

Why do you still want
the road that leads nowhere
but down.

Silence

Do not mistake
this lack of sound
for silence.

Silence is not a vacuum.
It is filled with
rhythms and sparks.

Growing Pains

You gave me a seed
tiny and dark

It sat curled in my palm
like a reproach
My visions of a
voluptuous harvest
stripped of the
imminent arrival
I had planned

High hopes grounded
in a parody
of the leaves that
would not be seen for months

I did not understand then
that the seed
was not the gift.

The Real You

The Real You
Is not what you think.

The Real You is huge, for one thing.
Endlessly expansive and pulsing with light.

The Real You
dances barefoot
sings loudly
laughs vibrantly into the sky
and delights in small things, like a child.

The Real You
is a firefly, a lighthouse, a sunray.
Rests in peace and lives in freedom.

The only reason
You don't know the truth of this
is because all your life
you have been putting on coats
that don't belong to you.

It's time to take the coats off now.
With this much sunshine,
even one is too many.

You are the lightworker
the wayshower
the one the world needs.

Show the world your light
and dazzle us all with the real reason you are here.
The Real You
reminds us how to shine.

Tara lives by the sea
in the south of England,
where she paints, writes and
offers online art based courses
with a focus on uncovering
and developing your unique creative self.

Find out more and
connect with her here:
www.taraleaver.com

Printed in Great Britain
by Amazon